Cheese Making

How to Make Various Cheeses at Home

Table of Contents

Introduction

What does fresh-baked lasagna have in common with a Monte Cristo sandwich? They are both loaded with delicious melted cheese. Cheese is the core ingredient in many different recipes from a wide variety of cultures and ethnicities. Every type of cheese is different but each and every one of them is delicious. If you fancy yourself a cheese lover, you may be curious to learn more about cheese making. You might be surprised to find that it is easier than you thought to create your own homemade cheese right in your own kitchen. If you are interested in cheese making, this book is the perfect place to start.

Within the pages of this book you will find a collection of twenty-five recipes for delicious cheeses including the basics like cream cheese, cottage cheese, and ricotta as well as flavored cheeses and several aged hard cheeses. So, if you are ready to try cheese making for yourself then simply pick a recipe from this book and get started!

Cheese Making Recipes

Recipes Included in this Book:

Simple Queso Fresco

Chipotle Queso Fresco

Homemade Cream Cheese

Garlic and Herb Cream Cheese

Labneh, or Yogurt Cheese

Toasted Walnut Labneh

Quick Homemade Ricotta

Cheddar Cheese

Fromage Blanc

Homemade Cottage Cheese

Fresh and Easy Mozzarella

Goat Cheese, or Chevre

Garlic and Basil Fromage Blanc

Feta Cheese

Monterey Jack Cheese

Sundried Tomato and Olive Cream Cheese

Roasted Garlic Labneh

Homemade Lemon Ricotta

Farmer's Cheese

Orange Zest and Toasted Pecan Chevre

Bacon Scallion Cream Cheese

Butterkase

Colby Cheese

Cranberry Almond Chevre

Garlic Rosemary Farmer's Cheese

Simple Queso Fresco

Ingredients:

- 4 quarts whole milk
- 2/3 cups distilled white vinegar
- Cheese salt to taste

Instructions:

1. Line a colander with a double layer of cheesecloth and place it over a large bowl.
2. Heat the milk in a large saucepan over medium-low heat, stirring often, until it reaches 180°F.
3. Whisk in the vinegar a few tablespoons at a time while stirring constantly until the curds begin to separate.

4. Remove from heat and let rest for 5 to 15 minutes until the separation is complete.
5. Spoon the curds into the lined colander and cover with plastic wrap.
6. Let drain for 20 minutes or so then stir in the salt.

Homemade Cream Cheese

Ingredients:

- 8 cups fresh cream
- 1 packet of direct-set mesophilic starter culture
- Cheese salt, to taste

Instructions:

1. Whisk together the cream and starter culture in a large bowl.
2. Cover the bowl with plastic and let rest for 12 hours until a solid curd forms.
3. Line a colander with cheesecloth then pour in the curd.
4. Gather up the corners of the cheesecloth into a bag and hang it over a bowl.

5. Let the cheese drain for 12 hours, changing the cheesecloth up to two times if needed.
6. Empty out the drained cheese into a bowl and stir in the salt. Use as desired.

Labneh, or Yogurt Cheese

Ingredients:

- 2 quarts whole milk
- 2 tablespoons plain yogurt (with live cultures)
- Cheese salt, as needed

Instructions:

1. Heat the milk in a large saucepan over medium-low heat, stirring often, until it reaches 180°F.
2. Remove from heat and let the milk cool to 110°F then whisk in the yogurt.
3. Cover the saucepan and maintain a temperature of 110°F to 8 to 12 hours.
4. Line a colander with a double layer of cheesecloth and place it over a large bowl.

5. Spoon the cheese into the lined colander and drain at room temperature for 12 to 24 hours.
6. Transfer the cheese to a bowl then stir in the salt and use as desired.

Quick Homemade Ricotta

Ingredients:

- 1 gallon whole milk
- ¼ cup cool water
- 1 teaspoon citric acid
- Cheese salt, to taste

Instructions:

1. Whisk together the water and citric acid in a small bowl.
2. Combine the milk with the citric acid solution in a large saucepan.
3. Slowly heat the mixture to about 190°F until the curds begin to separate from the whey.

4. Remove from heat and let rest for 10 minutes.
5. Line a colander with a double layer of cheesecloth and place it over a large bowl.
6. Spoon the cheese into the lined colander and drain at room temperature for about 30 to 45 minutes.
7. Transfer the cheese to a bowl then stir in the salt and use as desired.

Fromage Blanc

Ingredients:

- 1 gallon whole milk
- 1 packet fromage blanc starter culture

Instructions:

1. Heat the milk to 86°F in a large saucepan over medium heat.
2. Remove from heat and whisk in the starter culture using an up-and-down motion for no more than 30 seconds.
3. Cover the pot and let rest at a temperature of 72°F for 12 hours – the cheese should start to look like yogurt.
4. Line a colander with cheesecloth and place it over a large bowl.

5. Pour in the curds and whey then gather up the corners of the cheesecloth and tie it into a bag.
6. Hang the bag over the bowl and let drain for about 6 to 12 hours until it reaches the desired consistency.
7. Stir in the cheese salt, if desired, then store in the refrigerator.

Fresh and Easy Mozzarella

Ingredients:

- ½ cup cool water, divided
- 1 ½ teaspoons citric acid powder
- ¼ teaspoon liquid rennet
- 1 gallon whole milk
- Cheese salt, as needed

Instructions:

1. Whisk together ¼ cup of the water and citric acid in a small bowl.
2. In a separate bowl, whisk together the rennet with the remaining ¼ cup water.
3. Slowly heat the milk to about 55°F then whisk in the citric acid solution.

4. Continue to heat the mixture until it reaches 88°F – the milk will start to thicken to a yogurt-like consistency.
5. Slowly stir in the diluted rennet then stir continuously for 30 seconds.
6. Stop stirring and let the mixture heat to 105°F – the curds and whey should separate and start to pull away from the sides of the pot.
7. Remove from heat then spoon the curds into a cheesecloth-lined colander set over a large bowl.
8. Use a wooden spoon to press on the curds to remove as much whey as you can.
9. Pour the drained-off whey into a saucepan and heat to 175°F.
10. Shape the drained curds by hand into small balls by rolling the curds between your palms.
11. Dip the balls one at a time in the heated whey then knead them until the curds are warm and stretchy.
12. Continue kneading until the balls are smooth and very pliable then stir in the salt.
13. Serve the cheese warm or chill it in the refrigerator and serve within 1 week.

Goat Cheese, or Chevre

Ingredients:

- 1 gallon of goat's milk
- 1 packet chevre starter culture
- Cheese salt, as needed

Instructions:

1. Slowly heat the milk to about 68°F then sprinkle the starter culture over the milk.
2. Let the starter culture rehydrate for about 2 minutes then whisk it in.
3. Maintain the temperature and let the mixture sit for 6 to 12 hours until the curds start to coagulate.
4. When the curds and whey have separated and there is a clean break it is time to drain.

5. Line a colander with a double layer of cheesecloth and place it over a large bowl.
6. Spoon the cheese into the lined colander and drain at room temperature for about 6 hours.
7. Once the curds have drained properly, stir in the salt then store the cheese in a covered bowl in the refrigerator.

Chipotle Queso Fresco

Ingredients:

- 4 quarts whole milk
- 2/3 cups distilled white vinegar
- Cheese salt to taste
- 1 can chipotle chiles, drained and chopped
- 1 tablespoon adobo sauce (from canned chiles)

Instructions:

1. Line a colander with a double layer of cheesecloth and place it over a large bowl.
2. Heat the milk in a large saucepan over medium-low heat, stirring often, until it reaches 180°F.

3. Whisk in the vinegar a few tablespoons at a time while stirring constantly until the curds begin to separate.
4. Remove from heat and let rest for 5 to 15 minutes until the separation is complete.
5. Spoon the curds into the lined colander and cover with plastic wrap.
6. Let drain for 20 minutes or so then stir in the salt, chipotle peppers and adobo sauce.

Garlic and Herb Cream Cheese

Ingredients:

- 8 cups fresh cream
- 1 packet of direct-set mesophilic starter culture
- Cheese salt, to taste
- 2 cloves fresh minced garlic
- 1 teaspoon dried oregano
- 1 teaspoon dried parsley
- ½ teaspoon dried thyme
- ½ teaspoon dried basil

Instructions:

1. Whisk together the cream and starter culture in a large bowl.

2. Cover the bowl with plastic and let rest for 12 hours until a solid curd forms.
3. Line a colander with cheesecloth then pour in the curd.
4. Gather up the corners of the cheesecloth into a bag and hang it over a bowl.
5. Let the cheese drain for 12 hours, changing the cheesecloth up to two times if needed.
6. Empty out the drained cheese into a bowl and stir in the salt.
7. Add the garlic, oregano, parsley, thyme, and basil then stir well and use as desired.

Toasted Walnut Labneh

Ingredients:

- 2 quarts whole milk
- 2 tablespoons plain yogurt (with live cultures)
- Cheese salt, as needed
- ½ cup chopped walnut halves

Instructions:

1. Heat the milk in a large saucepan over medium-low heat, stirring often, until it reaches 180°F.
2. Remove from heat and let the milk cool to 110°F then whisk in the yogurt.
3. Cover the saucepan and maintain a temperature of 110°F to 8 to 12 hours.

4. Line a colander with a double layer of cheesecloth and place it over a large bowl.
5. Spoon the cheese into the lined colander and drain at room temperature for 12 to 24 hours.
6. Transfer the cheese to a bowl then stir in the salt.
7. Heat the oil in a small skillet over medium heat.
8. Add the walnuts and cook for 1 to 2 minutes until toasted.
9. Let the nuts cool slightly then stir them into the labneh and use as desired.

Cheddar Cheese

Ingredients:

- 2 gallons whole milk
- 1/8 teaspoon calcium chloride
- ¾ cups cold water, divided
- ½ teaspoon liquid rennet
- 1 packed direct-set mesophilic culture
- Cheese salt, to taste

Instructions:

1. In a small bowl, whisk together the calcium chloride with ¼ cup cold water.
2. In a separate bowl, whisk together the liquid rennet with the remaining ½ cup water.

3. Slowly heat the milk and calcium chloride to about 85°F then sprinkle the starter cultures over the milk.
4. Let the starter cultures rehydrate for about 2 minutes then whisk them in.
5. Cover the pot and maintain the temperature and let the mixture sit for 1 hour – the curd should start to pull away from the sides of the saucepan.
6. Cut the curds using a sharp knife into ¼-inch cubes and let sit for 5 minutes without stirring.
7. Slowly increase the temperature to 100°F while stirring often, increasing the temperature by 2°F every 5 minutes – it should take a total of about 30 minutes.
8. Allow the curds to settle for 30 minutes without stirring.
9. Strain the curds through a colander over the saucepan and let drain for 15 minutes.
10. Transfer the drained curds to a cutting board and cut into five slices.
11. Drain the whey from the pot and place the sliced curds in it then cover with the lid.
12. Place the pot in a water bath at 102° and maintain the temperature for 2 hours, turning the sliced curds every 15 minutes
13. Remove the curds after 2 hours and cut into ½-inch cubes then place them back in the pot and put the pot in the water bath.

14. Wait for 10 minutes then stir gently – repeat the process twice more.
15. Remove the pot from the water bath and stir in the salt.
16. Line a cheese press with cheesecloth then add the curds.
17. Press with 10 pounds of pressure for 15 minutes then urn and press with 40 pounds of pressure for 12 hours.
18. Turn the cheese and press with 50 pounds of pressure for 24 hours.
19. Remove and unwrap the cheese then let it air dry for 2 to 3 days, turning twice daily.
20. When the cheese forms a yellowish rind, wax the cheese then age at 40°F to 60°F for up to 6 months, turning once daily for the first month.

Homemade Cottage Cheese

Ingredients:

- 1 gallon skim milk, pasteurized
- ¾ cups distilled white vinegar
- 1 ½ teaspoons cheese salt
- ½ cup heavy cream, chilled

Instructions:

1. Heat the milk to 120°F in a large saucepan over medium heat.
2. Remove from heat and whisk in the vinegar.
3. Stir the mixture gently for 1 to 2 minutes until the curds start to separate from the whey.
4. Cover the pot and let rest at room temperature for 30 minutes.

5. Line a colander with cheesecloth and place it over a large bowl.
6. Pour in the curds and whey then let drain for about 5 minutes.
7. Gather up the corners of the cheesecloth and tie it into a bag then rinse with cool water for 3 to 5 minutes.
8. Squeeze the bag gently to remove as much moisture as possible then place the curds in a mixing bowl.
9. Stir in the salt, breaking the curds up into small pieces.
10. Refrigerate if desired then stir in the cream just before serving.

Garlic and Basil Fromage Blanc

Ingredients:

- 1 gallon whole milk
- 1 packet fromage blanc starter culture
- 1 tablespoon minced garlic
- 2 to 4 tablespoons fresh chopped basil

Instructions:

1. Heat the milk to 86°F in a large saucepan over medium heat.
2. Remove from heat and whisk in the starter culture using an up-and-down motion for no more than 30 seconds.
3. Cover the pot and let rest at a temperature of 72°F for 12 hours – the cheese should start to look like yogurt.

4. Line a colander with cheesecloth and place it over a large bowl.
5. Pour in the curds and whey then gather up the corners of the cheesecloth and tie it into a bag.
6. Hang the bag over the bowl and let drain for about 6 to 12 hours until it reaches the desired consistency.
7. Stir in the cheese salt, garlic, and basil then store in the refrigerator.

Feta Cheese

Ingredients:

- 1/8 teaspoon lipase powder
- ½ teaspoon calcium chloride liquid
- 8 tablespoons cold water, divided
- ¼ teaspoon feta mesophilic starter culture
- 1 gallon whole milk
- ½ gallon water
- 1 lbs. cheese salt

Instructions:

1. In a small bowl, whisk together the lipase powder with 2 tablespoons cold water.
2. In another bowl, combine the calcium chloride with 2 tablespoons cold water.

3. In a separate bowl, whisk together the liquid rennet with the remaining ¼ cup water.

4. Slowly heat the milk along with the calcium chloride mixture to about 90°F then remove from heat.

5. Sprinkle the starter cultures over the milk and let it rehydrate for 2 minutes before stirring it in.

6. Cut the curds using a sharp knife into ½-inch cubes and let sit for 5 minutes without stirring.

7. Cover the pot and maintain a temperature of 90°F for 20 minutes, allowing the curds to settle for the first 10 minutes.

8. Pour the curds and whey into a colander over the sink then divide the curds between two ricotta baskets.

9. Place one basket in a shallow dish then place the second basket on top.

10. Allow the curds to drain for 30 minutes then turn the curds and switch the baskets.

11. Press the curds for another 30 minutes, repeating the sequence two more times with 1 hour between switches.

12. Turn out the curds onto a draining mat and cover loosely with cheesecloth.

13. Let drain overnight at room temperature.

14. Prepare a brine using ½ gallon of water and 1 lbs. cheese salt.

15. Heat the brine until the salt is completely dissolved then cover and cool to room temperature.
16. Cut the cheese into 2-inch cubes and place them in the brine – refrigerate for 6 hours.
17. Remove the cheese and cut into blocks then store in jars filled with pickling brine.

Monterey Jack Cheese

Ingredients:

- 1 ½ teaspoons calcium chloride liquid
- 6 tablespoons cold water, divided
- ½ rennet tablet, crushed
- 3 gallons whole milk
- 2 cups heavy cream
- ¼ teaspoon mesophilic starter culture

Instructions:

1. In a small bowl, whisk together the calcium chloride with 2 tablespoons cold water.
2. In a separate bowl, whisk together the liquid rennet with the remaining 4 tablespoons cold water.

3. Slowly heat the milk, heavy cream, and the calcium chloride mixture to about 88°F in a double boiler.
4. Remove from heat then sprinkle the starter cultures over the milk.
5. Let the starter cultures rehydrate for about 2 minutes then whisk them in.
6. Cover the pot and maintain the temperature and let the mixture sit for 45 minutes – the curd should start to pull away from the sides of the saucepan.
7. Stir in the rennet mixture then let the milk sit, covered, at 88°F for 30 minutes or until it forms a clean break.
8. Cut the curds using a sharp knife into ½ inch cubes and let sit for 5 minutes without stirring.
9. Slowly increase the temperature to 100°F while stirring often, increasing the temperature by 2°F every 5 minutes – it should take a total of about 30 minutes.
10. Spoon off enough whey to bring it down to the surface level of the curds then allow the curds to settle for 30 minutes, stirring once every 5 minutes.
11. Drain the curds and whey in a large colander over the sink, stirring to remove as much moisture as possible.
12. Sprinkle the curds with 1 tablespoon salt then stir – wait 1 minute then repeat twice.

13. Line a cheese press with cheesecloth then add the curds.
14. Press with 5 pounds of pressure for 15 minutes then turn and press with 10 pounds of pressure for 12 hours.
15. Remove the cheese then whisk 1 tablespoon of salt with ½ cup water and brush it over the cheese.
16. Allow the cheese to air dry for 2 to 3 days, during twice daily.
17. When the cheese forms a yellowish rind, wax the cheese then age at 40°F to 60°F for up to 4 months, turning once daily for the first month.

Sundried Tomato and Olive Cream Cheese

Ingredients:

- 8 cups fresh cream
- 1 packet of direct-set mesophilic starter culture
- Cheese salt, to taste
- 8 to 12 sundried tomatoes, drained and diced
- ¼ cup pitted black olives, chopped

Instructions:

1. Whisk together the cream and starter culture in a large bowl.
2. Cover the bowl with plastic and let rest for 12 hours until a solid curd forms.
3. Line a colander with cheesecloth then pour in the curd.

4. Gather up the corners of the cheesecloth into a bag and hang it over a bowl.
5. Let the cheese drain for 12 hours, changing the cheesecloth up to two times if needed.
6. Empty out the drained cheese into a bowl and stir in the salt.
7. Add the sundried tomatoes and olives then stir well and use as desired.

Roasted Garlic Labneh

Ingredients:

- 2 quarts whole milk
- 2 tablespoons plain yogurt (with live cultures)
- Cheese salt, as needed
- ½ cup chopped walnut halves

Instructions:

1. Heat the milk in a large saucepan over medium-low heat, stirring often, until it reaches 180°F.
2. Remove from heat and let the milk cool to 110°F then whisk in the yogurt.
3. Cover the saucepan and maintain a temperature of 110°F to 8 to 12 hours.

4. Line a colander with a double layer of cheesecloth and place it over a large bowl.
5. Spoon the cheese into the lined colander and drain at room temperature for 12 to 24 hours.
6. Meanwhile, preheat the oven to 400°F and remove the outer peal from a head of garlic.
7. Trim the top ¼-inch off the top of the garlic and place it in a piece of foil.
8. Drizzle with olive oil then wrap the foil around the garlic.
9. Bake for 40 minutes or until soft then allow the garlic to cool slightly.
10. Remove the cloves from the head of garlic and chop them coarsely before using them.
11. Transfer the cheese to a bowl then stir in the salt and roasted garlic. Use as desired.

Homemade Lemon Ricotta

Ingredients:

- 1 gallon whole milk
- ¼ cup cool water
- 1 teaspoon citric acid
- 1 cup fresh squeezed lemon juice
- Cheese salt, to taste

Instructions:

1. Whisk together the water and citric acid in a small bowl.
2. Combine the milk with the citric acid solution in a large saucepan then whisk in the lemon juice.

3. Slowly heat the mixture to about 190°F until the curds begin to separate from the whey.
4. Remove from heat and let rest for 10 minutes.
5. Line a colander with a double layer of cheesecloth and place it over a large bowl.
6. Spoon the cheese into the lined colander and drain at room temperature for about 30 to 45 minutes.
7. Transfer the cheese to a bowl then stir in the salt and use as desired.

Farmer's Cheese

Ingredients:

- 1 gallon whole milk
- Juice from 1 lemon
- Cheese salt, as needed

Instructions:

1. Slowly bring the milk to a gentle boil in a large saucepan over medium heat.
2. When the milk starts to bubble, turn off the heat then whisk in the lemon juice.
3. Allow the milk to curdle for 5 to 10 minutes then stir in the salt.
4. Line a colander with a double layer of cheesecloth and set it over a large bowl.

5. Pour the cheese mixture into the colander and drain off the whey.
6. Gather up the corners of the cheesecloth into a bowl and squeeze out as much whey as possible.
7. Transfer the cheese to a clean bowl and cover with plastic then store in the refrigerator.

Orange Zest and Toasted Pecan Chevre

Ingredients:

- 1 gallon of goat's milk
- 1 packet chevre starter culture
- Cheese salt, as needed
- 1 tablespoon butter
- ½ cup chopped pecans
- 1 to 2 tablespoons fresh orange zest

Instructions:

1. Slowly heat the milk to about 68°F then sprinkle the starter culture over the milk.
2. Let the starter culture rehydrate for about 2 minutes then whisk it in.

3. Maintain the temperature and let the mixture sit for 6 to 12 hours until the curds start to coagulate.
4. When the curds and whey have separated and there is a clean break it is time to drain.
5. Line a colander with a double layer of cheesecloth and place it over a large bowl.
6. Spoon the cheese into the lined colander and drain at room temperature for about 6 hours.
7. Meanwhile, melt the butter in a medium skillet over medium-high heat.
8. Add the pecans and sauté for 2 to 3 minutes until toasted then drain on paper towels.
9. Once the curds have drained properly, stir in the salt, orange zest, and toasted pecans.
10. Store the cheese in a covered bowl in the refrigerator.

Bacon Scallion Cream Cheese

Ingredients:

- 8 cups fresh cream
- 1 packet of direct-set mesophilic starter culture
- Cheese salt, to taste
- ¼ lbs. cooked bacon, drained and chopped
- 1 to 2 scallions, sliced thin

Instructions:

1. Whisk together the cream and starter culture in a large bowl.
2. Cover the bowl with plastic and let rest for 12 hours until a solid curd forms.
3. Line a colander with cheesecloth then pour in the curd.

4. Gather up the corners of the cheesecloth into a bag and hang it over a bowl.
5. Let the cheese drain for 12 hours, changing the cheesecloth up to two times if needed.
6. Empty out the drained cheese into a bowl and stir in the salt. Use as desired.
7. Add the garlic, oregano, parsley, thyme, and basil then stir well and use as desired.

Butterkase

Ingredients:

- **Instructions**: 2 gallons of whole milk
- 1 packet thermophilic starter culture
- 1 packet buttermilk culture
- ½ teaspoon liquid rennet
- Cheese salt, as needed

Instructions:

1. Slowly heat the milk to about 86°F then sprinkle the starter cultures over the milk.
2. Let the starter cultures rehydrate for about 2 minutes then whisk them in.
3. Maintain the temperature and let the mixture sit for 45 to 60 minutes.

4. Line a cheese form with a double layer of cheesecloth and place it over a large bowl.
5. Heat the milk slowly to 104°F then stir in the liquid rennet for about 1 minute.
6. Let the mixture set for 20 to 25 minutes until thoroughly coagulated with a clean break.
7. Use a sharp knife to cut the curds vertically in both directions in 2-inch slices.
8. Let the curds rest for 5 minutes then cut horizontally with a spoon, breaking the curds up into pieces.
9. Once the curds are separated and cut, let them set for 15 to 30 minutes until they start to firm up – stir gently every 5 minutes.
10. Spoon out the whey until the level is about 1 inch below the surface of the curds.
11. Transfer the curds and whey to the prepared cheese form, compacting it gently.
12. Use a light weight (4 to 6 lbs.) to consolidate the curd for about 1 hour while keeping it warm – between 80°F and 90°F.
13. Remove, unwrap, turn, and rewrap the curds in the mold at 30 minute intervals over the next 4 to 5 hours.
14. Remove the cheese from the mold and cool overnight then transfer to a brine made from 1 gallon of water and 2 ¼ lbs. of cheese salt.

15. Let the cheese soak for 3 to 4 hours then remove the cheese to a flat surface and dry the surface.
16. Let the cheese dry for 24 hours then age for 4 to 6 weeks before serving.

Colby Cheese

Ingredients:

- 3 gallons of whole milk
- 1 ½ teaspoons calcium chloride
- ¼ teaspoon mesophilic starter culture
- ½ rennet tablet, crushed
- ¼ cup cold water
- 2 tablespoons cheese salt

Instructions:

1. Slowly heat the milk and calcium chloride to about 86°F then sprinkle the starter cultures over the milk.

2. Let the starter cultures rehydrate for about 2 minutes then whisk them in.
3. Cover the pot and maintain the temperature and let the mixture sit for 1 hour.
4. Whisk together the liquid rennet and water then stir into the milk.
5. Cover and let rest at 86°F for 30 to 40 minutes or until the curds form a clean break.
6. Use a sharp knife to cut the curds into ½-inch cubes then stir gently for about 5 minutes.
7. Slowly increase the temperature to 102°F, increasing the temperature by 2°F every 5 minutes – it should take a total of about 30 minutes.
8. Maintain the temperature at 102°F for 30 minutes, stirring gently every 5 minutes.
9. Cover the pot and let the curds settle for another 5 minutes.
10. Pour off enough whey to make it even with the surface of the curds.
11. Stir in enough cold water to reduce the temperature to 80°F then hold it at that temperature for 15 minutes while stirring.
12. Line a colander with cheesecloth and place it in the sink.
13. Pour in the curds and whey, stirring to drain more thoroughly, then stir in the salt one tablespoon at a time, letting the curds set for 1 minute after each addition.

14. Line a cheese press with cheesecloth then add the curds.
15. Press with 20 pounds of pressure for 20 minutes then urn and press with 30 pounds of pressure for 20 minutes.
16. Turn the cheese and press with 50 pounds of pressure for 12 hours.
17. Remove and unwrap the cheese then let it air dry for 2 to 3 days, during twice daily.
18. When the cheese forms a yellowish rind, wax the cheese then age at 40°F to 60°F for up to 6 months, turning once daily for the first month.

Cranberry Almond Chevre

Ingredients:

- 1 gallon of goat's milk
- 1 packet chevre starter culture
- Cheese salt, as needed
- 1 teaspoon butter
- ¼ cup chopped almonds
- 1 tablespoon raw honey
- ½ cup dried cranberries, chopped

Instructions:

1. Slowly heat the milk to about 68°F then sprinkle the starter culture over the milk.

2. Let the starter culture rehydrate for about 2 minutes then whisk it in.
3. Maintain the temperature and let the mixture sit for 6 to 12 hours until the curds start to coagulate.
4. When the curds and whey have separated and there is a clean break it is time to drain.
5. Line a colander with a double layer of cheesecloth and place it over a large bowl.
6. Spoon the cheese into the lined colander and drain at room temperature for about 6 hours.
7. Meanwhile, melt the butter in a medium skillet over medium-high heat.
8. Add the almonds and sauté for 2 to 3 minutes until toasted then drain on paper towels.
9. Once the curds have drained properly, stir in the salt, almonds, honey and cranberries.
10. Store the cheese in a covered bowl in the refrigerator.

Garlic Rosemary Farmer's Cheese

Ingredients:

- 1 gallon whole milk
- Juice from 1 lemon
- Cheese salt, as needed
- 1 tablespoon fresh minced garlic
- 2 sprigs fresh rosemary, chopped fine

Instructions:

1. Slowly bring the milk to a gentle boil in a large saucepan over medium heat.
2. When the milk starts to bubble, turn off the heat then whisk in the lemon juice.
3. Allow the milk to curdle for 5 to 10 minutes then stir in the salt.

4. Line a colander with a double layer of cheesecloth and set it over a large bowl.
5. Pour the cheese mixture into the colander and drain off the whey.
6. Gather up the corners of the cheesecloth into a bowl and squeeze out as much whey as possible.
7. Transfer the cheese to a clean bowl then stir in the garlic and rosemary.
8. Cover with plastic then store in the refrigerator.

Conclusion

If you are a fan of grilled-cheese sandwiches and homemade pizza then you are probably also a cheese lover. Rather than spending a small fortune on specialty cheeses at the grocery store, you might want to consider making some of your own cheeses at home! Cheese making is an enjoyable hobby that is surprisingly easy to pick up. Using the recipes in this book you can make everything from homemade ricotta and mozzarella to goat cheese, cheddar cheese, and Monterey jack. So, if you are ready to try cheese making for yourself then simply pick a recipe from this book and get started!

Made in United States
North Haven, CT
06 July 2023

38610516R00037